THE
MARTINI
GUIDE

THE
MARTINI
GUIDE
shaken and stirred

=== Steve Quirk ===

NEW
HOLLAND

CONTENTS

Introduction 7

Gin-based Martini Cocktails 21

Vodka-based Martini Cocktails 77

Glossary 138

Index 142

Introduction

This book has been designed for the lovers of martini cocktails and those who have yet to discover how to make them. Each recipe in this large collection is provided with clear and uncomplicated directions so that anyone can create a martini cocktail with ease. With 70 gin and vodka-based martini cocktail recipes at your fingertips, you will never be short of a martini recipe or two and are poised to host your own martini parties.

A martini is traditionally a gin-based cocktail although there are now just as many martini cocktails that are vodka-based. This book is divided into two sections – gin-based martini cocktails and vodka-based martini cocktails.

Approximate % alcohol volume (% alc/vol) content has been calculated and supplied for each drink in this book, as well as how many standard drinks each contains. These calculations are based on information obtained that is believed to be accurate and reliable, although they cannot be guaranteed due to % alc/vol variations between the different brands of spirits and liqueurs. These calculations should only be used as a guide. The % alc/vol for all spirits and liqueurs required for drinks contained within this book are provided in the glossary – if unsure then compare your spirits and liqueurs with the % alc/vol provided in the glossary.

◆ CONSTRUCTING A MARTINI ◆

Shaking – When ingredients are required to be shaken, half-fill a cocktail shaker with ice and then pour ingredients into the shaker over the ice. This will chill the ingredients quicker than pouring the ingredients into the shaker before ice. Avoid over-filling your cocktail shaker – leave room for shaking. To shake, stand still and shake vigorously for about ten seconds, strain into your chosen glass and serve or garnish. The majority of cocktail shakers have a strainer; if yours does not then you can use a Hawthorn strainer. Effervescent drinks should never be shaken in a cocktail shaker. Rinse shaker out thoroughly after each use and dry with a clean lint-free cloth. This will ensure that your drinks only have in them what they are supposed to and will not distort the flavour of the next drink that you prepare.

Stirring – Where ingredients are required to be stirred, half-fill a mixing glass with ice and pour the ingredients over the ice. Stir and strain into chosen glass. Usually ingredients that mix easily together are prepared in this manner.

✦ USEFUL TIPS ✦

Frosting – This is for the purpose of coating the rim of a glass with salt or sugar. This is achieved by moistening the rim of a glass using a slice of lemon or orange. Hold the chosen glass by its base or stem upside down and rest gently on a flat plate containing salt or caster sugar then twist slightly. If you press down on the glass too hard, this may result in chunks of salt or sugar sticking to the rim of glass. Lemon is used for salt-frosted rims and orange for sugar-frosted rims unless otherwise stated.

Ice – It is important to maintain a well-stocked clean ice supply, as most Martini cocktails require ice during construction.

To chill a glass – Glasses can be chilled by placing them into a refrigerator or by placing ice cubes into the glasses while drinks are being prepared. Discard these ice cubes before pouring unless otherwise instructed.

To frost a glass – Where ingredients are required to be poured into a frosted glass, these glasses can be frosted by placing them into a freezer prior to use.

Sugar syrup – To make sugar syrup, bring one cup of ordinary white sugar with one cup of water almost to boil in a small saucepan whilst stirring continuously, and simmer until sugar is completely dissolved. Remove from heat and allow to cool. Once cool, pour into a resealable container or a corked bottle and store in refrigerator or behind your bar for regular use. This syrup will now last indefinitely.

Fruit, peels and juices – Fruit slices and pieces will stay fresher and keep longer if covered with a damp clean linen cloth and refrigerated. Where citrus peel is required, cut the peel into required sizes and shave away the white membrane. Fruit and peels should be the last added ingredient to a cocktail (garnish). When juices are required remember – fresh is best. When using canned fruit and/or juices, transfer the contents into appropriate resealable containers and refrigerate.

◆ GLASSWARE ◆

Glasses come in a wide variety of shapes and sizes and range in value depending upon the quality of glass. When washing glasses, use hot water without detergent to avoid distorting the flavour of a drink. Only wash one glass at a time and dry with a clean lint-free cloth. Before using a glass, give it a quick polish with a glass cloth and check glass for chips and/ or cracks. When handling glassware, hold glasses by their base or stem as this will avoid finger marks around the rim of glass, thus maintaining a high polish.

The following is a list of glassware required for martini cocktails within this publication, although the majority of martini cocktails are served in a martini glass.

- **Brandy Balloon** 240 ml (8 fl oz) – 750 ml (26 fl oz)
- **Cocktail** 90 ml (3 fl oz) – 140 ml (4⅔ fl oz)
- **Martini** 90 ml (3 fl oz) – 1 ml (4⅔ fl oz)
- **Old-Fashioned** 180 ml (6 fl oz) – 290 ml (9⅔ fl oz)

```
                    MEASURES
        1 dash   1 ml (⅟₃₀ fl oz)
        1 teaspoon   5 ml (⅙ fl oz)
```

COMMON INGREDIENTS FOR MARGARITA COCKTAILS

Spirits
Gin
Southern Comfort
Vermouth
Vodka
Wiskey

Liqueurs
Banana Liqueur
Cointreau
Crème De Cacao
Crème De Menthe
Curaçao

Midori
Pernod
Sambuca
Strawberry Liqueur

COMMON MIXERS

- Apple Juice
- Lemon Juice
- Orange Juice
- Cranberry Juice
- Peach Nectar

- Spring Water
- Cherry Juice
- Lime Juice
- Pineapple Juice
- Raspberry Syrup

GARNISHES AND ADDITIVES

- Apricots
- Kiwi Fruit
- Peaches
- Sugar
- Bananas

- Lemons
- Salt and Pepper
- Blackberries
- Limes
- Strawberries

◆ HOSTING A MARTINI PARTY ◆

Being the host of a party can be stressful if you are not properly prepared. Here are some helpful hints to ensure that you and your guests enjoy the occasion.

It is advisable to pre-cut your fruit for garnishes and wrap them in plastic or place a clean damp linen cloth over them and refrigerate until required. Juices should be squeezed and/or removed from tin cans. Pour juices into resealable containers and refrigerate. Make up a bowl of sugar syrup as described under useful tips. This will save you from having to dissolve sugar when preparing large quantities of drinks. Keep a glass of water on your bar for rinsing instruments such as spoons and stirrers. If your washing machine is in close proximity to your bar or kitchen, it can be used to fill with clean fresh ice.

If you find yourself hosting a large party, it is an idea to make yourself a checklist of what you require and what must be completed. Once your list is all checked off, you should then be able to sit down and relax before your home is invaded by guests. Then you can enjoy sophisticated martini cocktails with family and friends without the stress of hosting the occasion.

◆ CORDIALS AND LIQUEURS ◆

Cordials and liqueurs are alcohol-based with herbs, aromatic plants, essences, juices, beans, nuts, dairy products, sweeteners and colors which are infused in the spirit by the process of steeping and distillation.

Traditionally, cordials and liqueurs were created for medicinal purposes as a cure for all types of ills. Creating cordials and liqueurs hundreds of years ago meant that people would gather herbs, fruits and plants from their gardens and then added them with sugar to liquors such as gin, brandy and other liquors. Today cordials and liqueurs are produced by distilling companies worldwide. It would not be possible to list all cordials and liqueurs that are being produced or available. A list has been provided of the main ones that are required for martini recipes in the introduction of this book. Cordials and liqueurs are essential ingredients in a vast variety of martini cocktails.

◆ MARTINI COCKTAILS ◆

The martini cocktail is a classic cocktail that originally consistered of gin and sweet vermouth.

It is not possible to be certain who created this cocktail or when it was created. There are several theories surrounding the martini that date back to the late 19th century and early 20th century.

One theory is that the martini cocktail was created by Martini di Arma di Taggia who was a bartender at Knickerbocker Hotel in New York in the early 20th century. This martini cocktail consisted of London dry gin, vermouth and orange bitters. Perhaps the martini cocktail was named after this bartender. Another theory is that the martini cocktail was named after the 'Martini & Rossi' brand name is an Italian Sweet Vermouth that was first produced in 1863. It is believed that patrons at bars would simply request a 'gin and martini'.

No matter what theory you lean towards believing, one thing is for sure, the martini cocktail has grown to become one of the world's best known cocktails and the varieties of martini cocktails continue to increase as the years go by.

Martini cocktails can range from very dry to sweet and are usually served chilled in a martini glass without a straw. They should be consumed by sipping slowly.

◆ ◆ ◆

Gin originated from Holland in the seventeenth century when a Dutch physician produced gin using juniper berries and alcohol for medicinal purposes.

Today gin is produced by distilling grain mash such as barley, corn and rye in column stills. This neutral spirit is then combined with water to reduce the strength before being redistilled with botanicals and aromatics. The botanicals and aromatics required for this procedure are primarily juniper berries and coriander. Other botanicals and aromatics that are used by distillers include bitter almonds, caraway seeds, cinnamon, fennel, ginger, lemon peel, orange peel, roots and other secret ingredients.

Gin is an unaged spirit with London Dry Gin being the most common type. Dry gin is produced by distillers around the world and contains no sugar.

COCKTAILS

BLUES MARTINI

36.6% alc/vol

0.9 standard drinks

15 ml (½ fl oz) dry gin

15 ml (½ fl oz) vodka

dash blue curaçao

Pour ingredients into a mixing glass over ice and stir gently. Strain into a martini glass over a small amount of cracked ice and serve.

PERFECT MARTINI

26.8% alc/vol

1.3 standard drinks

30 ml (1 fl oz) dry gin

15 ml (½ fl oz) dry vermouth

15 ml (½ fl oz) sweet vermouth

Pour ingredients into a mixing glass over ice and stir gently. Strain into a chilled martini glass and serve.

HOMESTEAD COCKTAIL

29.7% alc/vol

2.1 standard drinks

This drink is a Sweet Martini that is garnished with a slice of fresh orange – page 62.

BREAKFAST MARTINI NO.2

27.6% alc/vol
2 standard drinks

60 ml (2 fl oz) gin
15 ml (½ fl oz) strawberry liqueur
1 tablespoon orange marmalade

Pour gin and liqueur into a cocktail shaker over ice then add orange marmalade. Shake well and strain into a chilled martini glass then serve.

BLOODY MARTINI

27.8% alc/vol
1.4 standard drinks

45 ml (1½ fl oz) dry gin
5 ml (⅙ fl oz) dry vermouth
8 ml (¼ fl oz) grenadine
5 ml (⅙ fl oz) fresh lemon juice
fresh cherry
twist of fresh orange peel

Pour juice into a frosted martini glass and swirl around the glass then discard remainder of juice. Pour gin, vermouth and grenadine into a cocktail shaker over ice. Shake and strain into prepared glass. Garnish with a cherry and twist of orange peel then serve.

BURNT MARTINI

38% alc/vol
2.7 standard drinks

60 ml (2 fl oz) dry gin
30 ml (1 fl oz) blended whiskey

Pour ingredients into a martini glass without ice and stir gently then serve.

RACQUET CLUB MARTINI

33% alc/vol
2 standard drinks

60 ml (2 fl oz) gin
15 ml (½ fl oz) dry vermouth
2 dashes orange bitters

Pour ingredients into a mixing glass over ice and stir. Strain into a chilled martini glass and serve.

DICK DEMING MARTINI

32% alc/vol
1.9 standard drinks

60 ml (2 fl oz) gin
15 ml (½ fl oz) white wine

Pour ingredients into a mixing glass over ice and stir gently.
Strain into a chilled martini glass and serve.

STRAWBERRY MARTINI

33% alc/vol
1.8 standard drinks

60 ml (2 fl oz) gin
5 ml (⅙ fl oz) dry vermouth
5 ml (⅙ fl oz) grenadine
fresh strawberry

Prepare a martini glass with a sugar frosted rim – moistened with fresh strawberry juice. Pour gin, vermouth and grenadine into a mixing glass over ice then stir. Strain into prepared glass and add a strawberry then serve.

MARTINI ON THE ROCKS

36.1% alc/vol

1.9 standard drinks

60 ml (2 fl oz) dry gin

3 dashes dry vermouth

Pour ingredients into an old-fashioned glass half-filled with ice and stir then serve.

SMOKY MARTINI

36.5% alc/vol

1.5 standard drinks

50 ml (1⅔ fl oz) dry gin

dash dry dermouth

dash scotch whisky

Pour ingredients into a mixing glass over ice and stir. Strain into a frosted martini glass and serve.

MARTINI ESOTERICA

31% alc/vol

2.3 standard drinks

60 ml (2 fl oz) gin

30 ml (1 fl oz) dry vermouth

3 dashes Pernod

Pour ingredients into a cocktail shaker over ice and shake. Strain into a chilled martini glass and serve.

DRY MARTINI

33.8% alc/vol
2.4 standard drinks

75 ml (2½ fl oz) dry gin
15 ml (½ fl oz) dry vermouth
olive

Pour gin and vermouth into a mixing glass over ice then stir.
Strain into a chilled martini glass and add an olive then serve.

MARTIAN MARTINI

31.7% alc/vol

2.3 standard drinks

60 ml (2 fl oz) gin

30 ml (1 fl oz) Midori

Pour ingredients into a cocktail shaker over ice and shake. Strain into a chilled martini glass and serve.

PERNOD MARTINI

33.2% alc/vol

2 standard drinks

60 ml (2 fl oz) gin
15 ml (½ fl oz) dry vermouth
dash Pernod

Pour ingredients into a mixing glass over ice and stir. Strain into a chilled martini glass and serve.

MARTINI ORIENTAL

31.7% alc/vol
1.5 standard drinks

45 ml (1½ fl oz) gin
15 ml (½ fl oz) sake
twist of fresh lemon peel

Pour gin and sake into a mixing glass over ice then stir. Strain into a chilled martini glass and garnish with a twist of lemon peel then serve.

PAISLEY MARTINI

33.7% alc/vol
2.1 standard drinks

60 ml (2 fl oz) gin
15 ml (½ fl oz) dry vermouth
5 ml (⅙ fl oz) scotch whisky
twist of fresh lemon peel

Pour gin, vermouth and whisky into an old-fashioned glass half-filled with ice then stir. Garnish with a twist of lemon peel and serve.

HAWAIIAN MARTINI

31.4% alc/vol
2.2 standard drinks

60 ml (2 fl oz) dry gin
15 ml (½ fl oz) Cointreau
15 ml (½ fl oz) pineapple juice

Pour ingredients into a cocktail shaker over ice and shake.
Strain into a chilled martini glass and serve.

CHAMBORD MARTINI

30.2% alc/vol
2.1 standard drinks

60 ml (2 fl oz) gin
30 ml (1 fl oz) Chambord
twist of fresh lemon peel

Pour gin and Chambord into a cocktail shaker over ice then shake. Strain into a chilled martini glass and garnish with a twist of lemon peel then serve.

BALD HEAD MARTINI

30.3% alc/vol
2.2 standard drinks

60 ml (2 fl oz) gin
15 ml (½ fl oz) dry vermouth
15 ml (½ fl oz) sweet vermouth
2 dashes Pernod
twist of fresh lemon peel

Pour gin, vermouths and Pernod into a mixing glass over ice then stir gently. Strain into a martini glass over small amount of cracked ice and garnish with a twist of lemon peel then serve.

BLACK MARTINI

37.4% alc/vol

0.9 standard drinks

20 ml (⅔ fl oz) gin

10 ml (⅔ fl oz) black sambuca

Pour ingredients into a mixing glass over ice and stir. Strain into a chilled martini glass and serve.

BLUE MOON MARTINI

33% alc/vol
1.8 standard drinks

45 ml (1½ fl oz) dry gin
23 ml (¾ fl oz) blue curaçao
wedge of fresh lemon

Pour gin and curaçao into a mixing glass over ice then stir. Strain into a chilled martini glass and garnish with a wedge of lemon then serve.

SAKETINI

33.4% alc/vol
2.4 standard drinks

75 ml (2½ fl oz) dry gin
15 ml (½ fl oz) sake
twist of fresh lemon peel

Pour gin and sake into a mixing glass over ice then stir. Strain into a chilled martini glass and garnish with a twist of lemon peel then serve.

IMPERIAL MARTINI

27.7% alc/vol

1.4 standard drinks

30 ml (1 fl oz) dry gin

30 ml (1 fl oz) dry vermouth

dash angostura bitters

dash maraschino liqueur

olive

Pour gin, vermouth, bitters and liqueur into a mixing glass over ice then stir. Strain into a chilled martini glass and garnish with an olive then serve.

HARRY DENTON MARTINI

42.1% alc/vol

1.8 standard drinks

38 ml (1¼ fl oz) gin

15 ml (½ fl oz) Green Chartreuse

Pour ingredients into a cocktail shaker over ice and shake. Strain into a chilled martini glass and serve.

GUNGA DIN MARTINI

23.4% alc/vol

1.5 standard drinks

45 ml (1½ fl oz) gin
15 ml (½ fl oz) dry vermouth
23 ml (¾ fl oz) fresh orange juice
slice of fresh pineapple

Pour gin, vermouth and juice into a cocktail shaker over ice then shake. Strain into a chilled martini glass and garnish with a slice of pineapple then serve.

SWEET MARTINI

29.7% alc/vol
2.1 standard drinks

60 ml (2 fl oz) gin
30 ml (1 fl oz) sweet vermouth
maraschino cherry

Pour gin and vermouth into a mixing glass over ice then stir. Strain into a chilled martini glass and add a maraschino cherry then serve.

SAND MARTINI

27.5% alc/vol
2.1 standard drinks

45 ml (1½ fl oz) dry gin
45 ml (1½ fl oz) sweet vermouth
5 ml (⅙ fl oz) Green Chartreuse

Pour ingredients into a mixing glass over ice and stir. Strain into a chilled martini glass and serve.

EMERALD MARTINI

33.3% alc/vol
1.7 standard drinks

45 ml (1½ fl oz) gin
15 ml (½ fl oz) dry vermouth
3 dashes Green Chartreuse
twist of fresh lemon peel

Pour gin, vermouth and Chartreuse into a mixing glass over ice. Stir and strain into a chilled martini glass. Twist lemon peel above drink and place remainder of peel into drink then serve.

SOUTHERN MARTINI

33.3% alc/vol
2.4 standard drinks

60 ml (2 fl oz) gin
15 ml (½ fl oz) Southern Comfort
15 ml (½ fl oz) sweet vermouth
maraschino cherry

Pour gin, Southern Comfort and vermouth into a mixing glass over ice then stir. Strain into a chilled martini glass and garnish with a maraschino cherry then serve.

MARTINI EXOTICA

26.4% alc/vol
1.6 standard drinks

45 ml (1½ fl oz) dry gin
15 ml (½ fl oz) Midori
15 ml (½ fl oz) fresh lime juice
slice of fresh lime

Pour gin, Midori and juice into a mixing glass over ice then stir. Strain into a chilled martini glass and garnish with a slice of lime then serve.

ROUGE MARTINI

35.5% alc/vol
1.8 standard drinks

60 ml (2 fl oz) gin
5 ml (⅙ fl oz) Chambord

Pour ingredients into a mixing glass over ice and stir gently.
Strain into a chilled martini glass and serve.

MINT MARTINI

32.4% alc/vol
2.3 standard drinks

60 ml (2 fl oz) gin
30 ml (1 fl oz) green crème de menthe
3 fresh mint leaves

Pour gin and crème de menthe into a mixing glass over ice then stir. Strain into a chilled martini glass and garnish with mint leaves then serve.

FINO MARTINI

34.3% alc/vol

1.9 standard drinks

60 ml (2 fl oz) gin

10 ml (⅓ fl oz) fino sherry

twist of fresh lemon peel

Pour gin and sherry into a mixing glass over ice then stir. Strain into a chilled martini glass and add a twist of lemon peel then serve.

THE CAPTAIN'S MARTINI

32.3% alc/vol
1.7 standard drinks

45 ml (1½ fl oz) gin
15 ml (½ fl oz) white crème de menthe
5 ml (⅙ fl oz) dry vermouth

Pour ingredients into a cocktail shaker over ice and shake.
Strain into a chilled martini glass and serve.

◆ ◆ ◆

Vodka originated from Eastern Europe around the fourteenth century, perhaps even earlier. Traditional Russian Vodka is distilled from potatoes with fruit or herbs added during the distilling process to provide a hint of flavour to the vodka.

Vodka translates as 'little water'.

In the western nations, vodka is distilled from grain to a neutral spirit and filtered through charcoal leaving a clear spirit with little or no scent or taste.

Vodkas are now being produced by distilling companies with flavours added such as: lemon, lime and other fruits as well as varieties like pepper and chilli vodkas.

Vodka is now also being utilized as the main ingredient in martini cocktails, replacing the traditional main ingredient of gin.

COCKTAILS

VODKA MARTINI

33.8% alc/vol
2.4 standard drinks

75 ml (2½ fl oz) vodka
15 ml (½ fl oz) dry vermouth
twist of fresh lemon peel

Pour vodka and vermouth into a mixing glass over ice then stir. Strain into a chilled martini glass and garnish with a twist of lemon peel then serve.

BLUE MARTINI

22.6% alc/vol
1.5 standard drinks

45 ml (1½ fl oz) vodka
10 ml (⅔ fl oz) blue curaçao
10 ml (⅔ fl oz) fresh lemon juice
4 fresh blueberries (diced)
1 fresh blueberry

Place diced blueberries into a cocktail shaker without ice and muddle well then add ice. Add vodka, curaçao and juice then shake well to combine the ingredients. Strain into a chilled martini glass and garnish with a blueberry then serve.

EMERALD VODKA MARTINI

33.3% alc/vol
1.7 standard drinks

45 ml (1½ fl oz) vodka
15 ml (½ fl oz) dry vermouth
3 dashes Green Chartreuse
twist of fresh lemon peel

Pour vodka, vermouth and Chartreuse into a mixing glass over ice. Stir gently and strain into a chilled martini glass. Twist lemon peel above drink and place remainder of peel into drink then serve.

CHOCOLATE BANANA MARTINI

30% alc/vol
1.9 standard drinks

40 ml (1⅓ fl oz) vodka
20 ml (⅔ fl oz) banana liqueur
20 ml (⅔ fl oz) white crème de cacao

Pour ingredients into a mixing glass over ice and stir gently.
Strain into a chilled martini glass and serve.

COMFORTABLE MARTINI

37% alc/vol

2.9 standard drinks

90 ml (3 fl oz) honey vodka

8 ml (¼ fl oz) Southern Comfort

Pour ingredients into a mixing glass over ice and stir. Strain into a chilled cocktail glass and serve.

EURO-TINI

17.2% alc/vol

0.7 standard drinks

10 ml (⅓ fl oz) vodka
8 ml (¼ fl oz) Cointreau
8 ml (¼ fl oz) red curaçao
23 ml (¾ fl oz) fresh orange juice
½ teaspoon sugar syrup

Pour ingredients into a cocktail shaker over ice and shake. Strain into a chilled martini glass and serve.

BREAKFAST MARTINI

34.2% alc/vol
1.8 standard drinks

60 ml (2 fl oz) vodka
1 teaspoon marmalade

Pour vodka into a cocktail shaker over ice and add marmalade.
Shake well and strain into a chilled martini glass then serve.

BERLIN MARTINI

36.3% alc/vol
1.9 standard drinks

60 ml (2 fl oz) vodka
5 ml (⅙ fl oz) Opal Nera
3 dashes peach schnapps
fresh blackberry

Pour vodka, Opal Nera and schnapps into a cocktail shaker over ice then shake. Strain into a chilled martini glass and garnish with a blackberry then serve.

ALTERNATINI

31.1% alc/vol
2.2 standard drinks

60 ml (2 fl oz) vodka
15 ml (½ fl oz) white crème de cacao
8 ml (¼ fl oz) dry vermouth
8 ml (¼ fl oz) sweet vermouth

Pour ingredients into a mixing glass over ice and stir. Strain into a chilled martini glass and serve.

CHOCOLATE MARTINI

34.2% alc/vol
2 standard drinks

60 ml (2 fl oz) vodka
15 ml (½ fl oz) white crème de cacao

Pour ingredients into a cocktail shaker over ice and shake.
Strain into a chilled martini glass and serve.

This drink is also known as Chocolate Monk.

SURFER'S MARTINI

24.6% alc/vol
1.8 standard drinks

60 ml (2 fl oz) citrus vodka
dash dry vermouth
30 ml (1 fl oz) fresh lemon juice

Pour vermouth into a chilled martini glass and swirl around the glass. Add vodka and stir. Add juice and stir well then serve.

ALTERN-A-TINI

15.5% alc/vol

0.6 standard drinks

10 ml (⅓ fl oz) vodka

10 ml (⅓ fl oz) red curaçao

5 ml (⅙ fl oz) blue curaçao

23 ml (¾ fl oz) apple juice

Pour ingredients into a cocktail shaker over ice and shake. Strain into a chilled martini glass and serve.

CHOCOLATE MINT MARTINI

31% alc/vol
2.6 standard drinks

60 ml (2 fl oz) vodka
30 ml (1 fl oz) white crème de cacao
30 ml (1 fl oz) white crème de menthe

Prepare a cocktail glass with a cocoa powder frosted rim – moistened with cacao. Pour ingredients into a cocktail shaker over ice and shake. Strain into prepared glass and serve.

COSMOPOLITAN MARTINI

26.3% alc/vol

1.3 standard drinks

30 ml (1 fl oz) vodka
15 ml (½ fl oz) Cointreau
15 ml (½ fl oz) fresh lime juice
5 ml (⅙ fl oz) cranberry juice

Pour ingredients into a cocktail shaker over ice and shake.
Strain into a chilled martini glass and serve.

BRAZEN MARTINI

34.2% alc/vol
2 standard drinks

60 ml (2 fl oz) vodka
15 ml (½ fl oz) parfait amour
2 dried cranberries

Place dried cranberries into a chilled martini glass then pour vodka and parfait amour into a mixing glass over ice. Stir and strain into the glass over cranberries then serve.

MONK'S MARTINI

25.1% alc/vol
1.6 standard drinks

20 ml (⅔ fl oz) vodka
20 ml (⅔ fl oz) Bailey's Irish Cream
20 ml (⅔ fl oz) banana liqueur
20 ml (⅔ fl oz) white crème de menthe

Pour ingredients into a mixing glass over ice and stir. Strain into a chilled martini glass and serve.

DEWBERRY MARTINI

14.4% alc/vol
1 standard drink

23 ml (¾ fl oz) vodka
15 ml (½ fl oz) blue curaçao
dash dry vermouth
45 ml (1½ fl oz) cranberry juice

Pour ingredients into a mixing glass over ice and stir. Strain into a chilled martini glass and serve.

SAM-TINI

36.8% alc/vol
1.2 standard drinks

38 ml (1¼ fl oz) vodka
3 dashes white sambuca
dash blue curaçao
wedge of fresh orange

Pour vodka, sambuca and curaçao into a mixing glass over ice then stir. Strain into a chilled martini glass and garnish with a wedge of orange then serve.

BELLINI MARTINI

23.5% alc/vol
3.3 standard drinks

90 ml (3 fl oz) vodka
45 ml (1½ fl oz) peach schnapps
45 ml (1½ fl oz) peach nectar
twist of fresh lemon peel

Pour vodka, schnapps and nectar into a cocktail shaker over ice then shake well. Strain into a chilled brandy balloon and add a twist of lemon peel then serve.

FRENCH MARTINI

30.2% alc/vol

1.8 standard drinks

45 ml (1½ fl oz) vodka

30 ml (1 fl oz) black raspberry liqueur

Pour ingredients into a mixing glass over ice and stir. Strain into a chilled martini glass and serve.

VODKA MARTINI SWEET

28.2% alc/vol

1.7 standard drinks

45 ml (1½ fl oz) vodka

30 ml (1 fl oz) sweet vermouth

Pour ingredients into a mixing glass over ice and stir. Strain into a chilled martini glass and serve.

CHOCOLATE MONK

34.2% alc/vol
2 standard drinks

This drink is also known as Chocolate Martini – page 93.

BUCKEYE MARTINI

35% alc/vol
2.1 standard drinks

68 ml (2¼ fl oz) vodka
8 ml (¼ fl oz) dry vermouth
black olive

Pour vodka and vermouth into a mixing glass over ice then stir. Strain into a chilled martini glass and add a black olive then serve.

VIOLET MARTINI

31% alc/vol
2 standard drinks

60 ml (2 fl oz) citrus vodka
15 ml (½ fl oz) parfait amour
1½ teaspoons raspberry syrup

Pour ingredients into a mixing glass over ice and stir well.
Strain into a chilled martini glass and serve.

CHAMTINI

28.1% alc/vol

1.2 standard drinks

30 ml (1 fl oz) vodka

23 ml (¾ fl oz) Chambord

wedge of fresh lemon

Pour vodka and Chambord into a mixing glass over ice then stir. Strain into a chilled martini glass and add a wedge of lemon then serve.

MORTINI

36.6% alc/vol
1.8 standard drinks

60 ml (2 fl oz) vodka
2 drops amaretto
2 drops grenadine

Pour amaretto and grenadine into a chilled martini glass – do not stir, then swirl around the glass. Pour vodka into a mixing glass over ice and stir to chill. Strain into prepared glass – do not stir, then serve.

HAZELNUT MARTINI

32.7% alc/vol

1.2 standard drinks

30 ml (1 fl oz) vodka

15 ml (½ fl oz) Frangelico

Pour ingredients into a mixing glass over ice and stir. Strain into a chilled martini glass and serve.

ECCENTRIC EMAILER MARTINI

22.8% alc/vol

1.3 standard drinks

30 ml (1 fl oz) vodka

30 ml (1 fl oz) Kahlúa

15 ml (½ fl oz) spring water

Pour ingredients into a cocktail shaker over ice and shake. Strain into a chilled martini glass and serve.

KIWI MARTINI

18.4% alc/vol
1.8 standard drinks

60 ml (2 fl oz) vodka
dash sugar syrup
1 fresh kiwi fruit pulp (crushed)
slice of fresh kiwi fruit

Pour vodka and sugar into a cocktail shaker over ice then add crushed kiwi fruit. Shake well and strain into a chilled martini glass. Garnish with a slice of kiwi fruit and serve.

CASTRO MARTINI

35.4% alc/vol
1.4 standard drinks

45 ml (1½ fl oz) vodka
5 ml (⅙ fl oz) Pisang Ambon

Pour ingredients into a cocktail shaker over ice and shake.
Strain into a chilled martini glass and serve.

RUSSIAN PEACHTINI

35.3% alc/vol
1.4 standard drinks

45 ml (1½ fl oz) russian vodka
5 ml (⅙ fl oz) peach schnapps

Pour ingredients into a mixing glass over ice and stir. Strain into a chilled martini glass and serve.

WATERMELON MARTINI

31.6% alc/vol
1.9 standard drinks

60 ml (2 fl oz) vodka
dash sugar syrup
slice of fresh watermelon (crushed)
wedge of fresh watermelon

Pour vodka and sugar into a cocktail shaker over ice then add crushed watermelon. Shake well and strain into a chilled martini glass. Garnish with a wedge of watermelon and serve.

CHERRY MARTINI

27.2% alc/vol

1.9 standard drinks

60 ml (2 fl oz) vodka
15 ml (½ fl oz) sweet vermouth
15 ml (½ fl oz) cherry juice
2 maraschino cherries

Pour vodka, vermouth and juice into a cocktail shaker over ice then shake. Strain into a chilled martini glass and garnish with maraschino cherries then serve.

VODKA MARTINI MEDIUM

28.8% alc/vol
1.7 standard drinks

45 ml (1½ fl oz) vodka
15 ml (½ fl oz) dry vermouth
15 ml (½ fl oz) sweet vermouth

Pour ingredients into a mixing glass over ice and stir. Strain
into a chilled martini glass and serve.

BLUE SKY MARTINI

35.6% alc/vol

1.9 standard drinks

60 ml (2 fl oz) vodka

8 ml (¼ fl oz) blue curaçao

Pour ingredients into a mixing glass over ice and stir gently. Strain into a chilled martini glass and serve.

Glossary

Amaretto Almond-flavour liqueur that originated from Italy in 1525. **28**

Angostura Bitters Produced with infusions of herbs; it is the Bitters that gives Pink Gin its colour. **45**

Bailey's Irish Cream Brand name of a slight chocolate-flavour Irish cream liqueur produced with a blend of Irish Whiskey and fresh cream. **17**

Banana Liqueur Banana-flavour liqueur. **23**

Black Raspberry Liqueur Black raspberry-flavour liqueur produced from framboise – small black raspberries. **20**

Chambord Black raspberry-flavour liqueur produced in the Burgundy region of France **16.5**

Chartreuse (Green) Herbal liqueur produced in France **55**

Cointreau Sweet orange-flavour liqueur that is colourless and arguably the Worlds' finest Triple Sec. It has been produced by the Cointreau family in France since 1849. **40**

Crème De Cacao Chocolate and vanilla-flavour liqueur produced from cocoa beans, vanilla and spices. It is available in two varieties: dark and white (clear). **23**

Crème De Menthe Peppermint-flavour liqueur produced in three varieties: green, red and white (clear). **23**

Curaçao Sweet orange-flavour liqueur produced from curaçao orange peel. It is available in six varieties: blue, green, orange, red, white (clear) and yellow. **25**

Frangelico Hazelnut-flavour liqueur created by a monk over three hundred years ago in the Piedmont region of Italy. **24**

Grenadine Sweet red syrup, flavoured with pomegranate juice. **Nil**

Gin Colourless spirit produced from juniper berries and other botanicals. Gin is the most widely required spirit in cocktails. **37**

Kahlúa Coffee-flavour liqueur that is produced in Mexico. **20**

Maraschino Liqueur Cherry-flavour clear liqueur that originated in Italy. **40**

Midori Brand name of a honeydew melon-flavour liqueur that is green in colour and produced by the Suntory Distilling Company in Japan. **21**

Opal Nera Brand name of an aniseed-flavour Black Sambuca..................... 38

Orange Bitters Orange-flavour liqueur that is bitter-sweet and dry. It is produced from the peel of seville oranges... 26

Parfait Amour Citrus and rose scented, violet colour liqueur. Produced from Brandy, citrus and herbs it originated from France................................... 23

Pernod Aniseed-flavour liqueur originally produced in France as a substitute for Absinthe.. 40

Pisang Ambon Banana and herb-flavour liqueur originating from Indonesia and is produced from the tropical fruits and herbs of South-East Asia.............. 21

Sake Japanese brew fermented from rice, it may be served chilled or warm................... 15.5

Sambuca Aniseed-flavour liqueur produced from aniseed, herbs and roots. This liqueur is produced in Italy... 38

Schnapps Generic name for flavoured alcohol that is produced from grain or potato mash. Schnapps can be very sweet through to dry with many varieties available. % alc/vol content varies between the varieties. 20% alc/vol is average for commercial Schnapps.. 20

Sherry Produced from grapes and fortified with Brandy. True Sherry originates from Jerez in southern Spain... 18

Southern Comfort Peach-flavour liqueur that is Brandy and Bourbon-based. Created by M.W. Heron in New Orleans over one hundred years ago.................. 37

Strawberry Liqueur Strawberry-flavour liqueur.. 23

Vermouth (Dry) A Fortified Wine-based apéritif produced from herbs, flowers and roots... 18

Vermouth (Sweet)... 15

Vodka Clear, odourless and tasteless spirit distilled from fermented grain mash and filtered through charcoal. Traditional Russian and Polish Vodkas have subtle aromas and flavours... 37

Whiskey Spirit distilled from grain and then aged. They are produced in blends and single malts... 40

Index

A

Altern-a-Tini 96
Alternatini 92

B

Bald Head Martini 51
Bellini Martini 108
Berlin Martini 41
Black Martini 53
Bloody Martini 29
Blue Martini 81
Blue Moon Martini 55
Blue Sky Martini 137
Blues Martini 23
Brazen Martini 103
Breakfast Martini 89
Breakfast Martini No.2 27
Buckeye Martini 115
Burnt Martini 31

C

Castro Martini 127
Chambord Martini 50
Chamtini 118
Cherry Martini 133
Chocolate Banana Martini 83

Chocolate Martini 93
Chocolate Mint Martini 98
Chocolate Monk 113
Comfortable Martini 84
Cosmopolitan Martini 99

D

Dewberry Martini 106
Dick Deming Martini 33
Dry Martini 41

E

Eccentric Emailer Martini 112
Emerald Martini 64
Emerald Vodka Martini 82
Euro-Tini 86

F

Fino Martini 73
French Martini 110

G

Gunga Din Martini 61

H

Harry Denton Martini 59

Hawaiian Martini 48
Hazelnut Martini 120
Homestead Cocktail 26

I
Imperial Martini 57

K
Kiwi Martini 125

M
Martian Martini 43
Martini Esoterica 39
Martini Exotica 68
Martini on the Rocks 36
Martini Oriental 45
Mint Martini 71
Monk's Martini 105
Mortini 119

P
Paisley Martini 46
Perfect Martini 25
Pernod Martini 44

R
Racquet Club Martini 32
Rouge Martini 69
Russian Peachtini 128

S
Saketini 56
Sam-Tini 107
Sand Martini 63
Smoky Martini 38
Southern Martini 66
Strawberry Martini 34
Sweet Martini 62
Surfer's Martini 94

T
The Captain's Martini 74

V
Violet Martini 117
Vodka Martini 79
Vodka Martini Medium 135
Vodka Martini Sweet 112

W
Watermelon Martini 130

First published in 2017 by New Holland Publishers
London • Sydney • Auckland

The Chandlery 50 Westminster Bridge Road London SE1 7QY United Kingdom
1/66 Gibbes Street Chatswood NSW 2067 Australia
5/39 Woodside Ave Northcote Auckland 0627 New Zealand

www.newhollandpublishers.com

A record of this book is held at the British Library and the National Library of Australia.

ISBN 9781742579573

Group Managing Director: Fiona Schultz
Publisher: Alan Whiticker
Project Editor: Sarah Menary
Designer: Lorena Susak
Proofreader: Kaitlyn Smith
Production Director: James Mills-Hicks
Special thanks to Chris Howley for making the cocktails
Printer: Hang Tai Printing Company Limited

10 9 8 7 6 5 4 3 2 1

Keep up with New Holland Publishers on Facebook
www.facebook.com/NewHollandPublishers